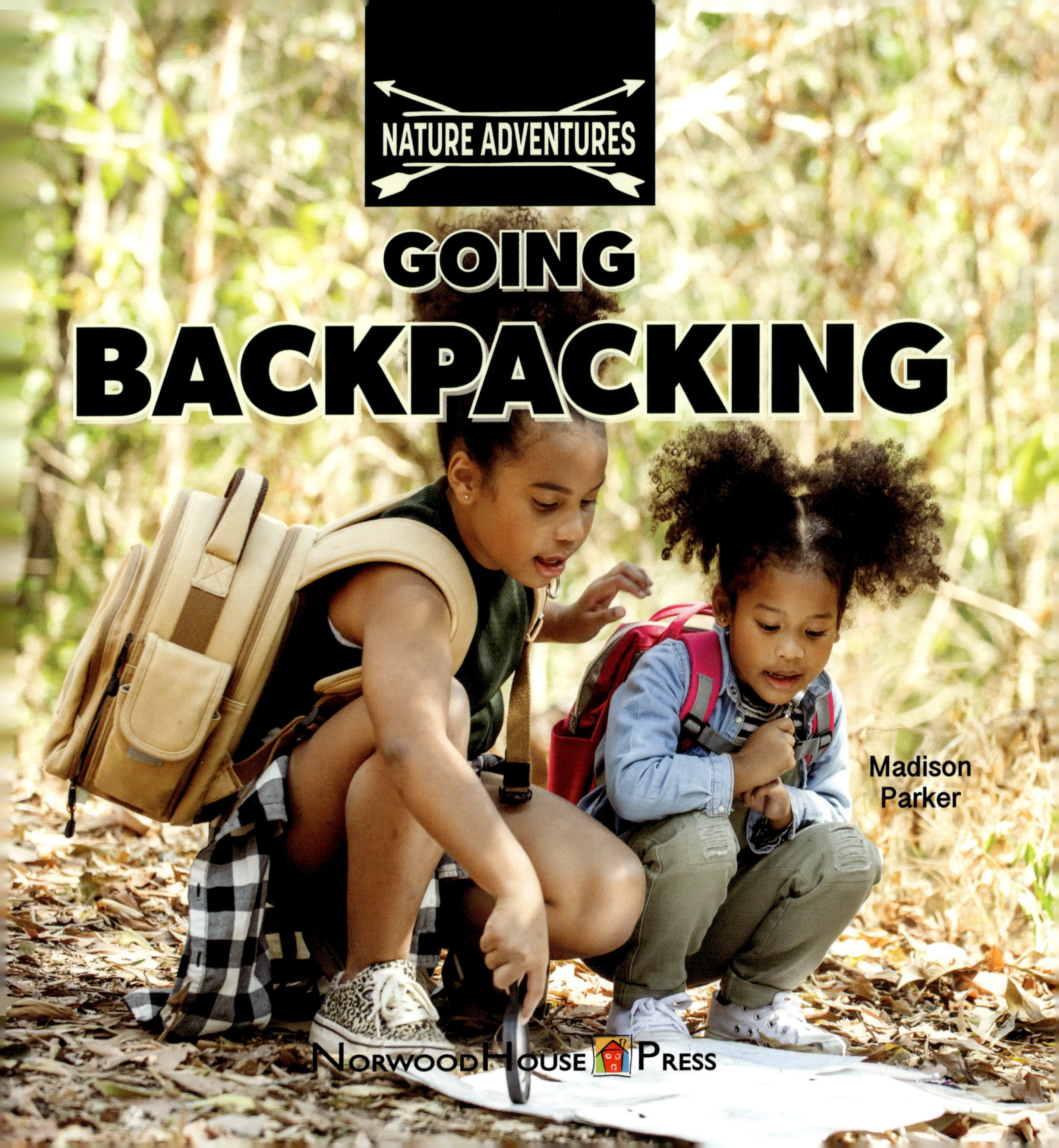
NATURE ADVENTURES
GOING
BACKPACKING
Madison
Parker
NORWOOD HOUSE PRESS

Cataloging-in-Publication Data

Names: Parker, Madison.
Title: Going backpacking / Madison Parker.
Description: Buffalo, NY : Norwood House Press, 2026. | Series: Nature adventures | Includes glossary and index.
Identifiers: ISBN 9781978574564 (pbk.) | ISBN 9781978574571 (library bound) | ISBN 9781978574588 (ebook)
Subjects: LCSH: Backpacking--Juvenile literature. | Hiking--Juvenile literature.
Classification: LCC GV199.6 P375 2026 | DDC 796.51--dc23

Published in 2026 by
Norwood House Press
2544 Clinton Street
Buffalo, NY 14224

Designer: Rhea Magaro
Editor: Kim Thompson

Photo credits: Cover, p. 1 CandyRetriever/Shutterstock.com; p. 5 everst/Shutterstock.com; p. 6 Pressmaster/Shutterstock.com; p. 7 Roberto Caucino/Shutterstock.com; p. 8 NAR studio/Shutterstock.com; pp. 9,21 Monkey Business Images/Shutterstock.com; pp. 10, 11 simoly/Shutterstock.com; p. 13 Ivanko80/Shutterstock.com; p. 14 PH888/Shutterstock.com; p. 17 Terry Kelly/Shutterstock.com; p. 18 Lungkhaek/Shutterstock.com; p. 19 Frank Fischbach/Shutterstock.com;

Printed in the United States of America

CPSIA compliance information: Batch #CSNHP26: For further information contact Norwood House Press at 1-800-237-9932.

TABLE OF CONTENTS

WHAT IS BACKPACKING?

Let's go backpacking! Backpacking is a fun outdoor activity.

Backpacking is when people hike for more than one day. They sleep outside. They carry all the supplies they need on their backs.

Many people enjoy backpacking adventures. They get away from their ordinary lives. They are surrounded by nature. There is a lot to see!

BACKPACKING SUPPLIES

You will need a backpack specially made for backpacking. It must have many **compartments** to hold all your gear.

When it is full, your backpack will be heavy. Straps and buckles help **distribute** the weight over your body.

Be **strategic** when you fill your backpack. Pack only what you really need. This will limit the weight you have to carry.

Bring the same supplies you would take on a camping trip. This includes a tent or other **shelter**, a sleeping bag, and food.

Dress in layers. This will keep you comfortable in different types of weather. Wear strong boots for walking over rough ground.

BACKPACKING SAFETY

It is important to stay safe when you go backpacking. It is a tiring activity. Take frequent breaks. Allow time for rest. Drink plenty of water.

Backpackers should Leave No **Trace** (LNT). That means you should not leave trash or anything else behind. Leave the **wilderness** better than you found it. This protects **wildlife**.

Treat
YUMMY

WHERE TO GO BACKPACKING

There are many great places for backpacking. There are trails that go through forests, mountains, **canyons**, and more.

Make sure to read any **regulations** before you go. It is a good idea to **reserve** campsites in advance.

You can visit your state's park website to find trails near you. Backpacking helps you explore the great outdoors!

Glossary

canyons (KAN-yuhnz): deep, narrow river valleys with steep sides

compartments (kuhm-PAHRT-muhnts): separate areas for keeping different things inside the same container

distribute (di-STRIB-yoot): to spread out equally

regulations (reg-yuh-LAY-shuhnz): rules you need to follow

reserve (ri-ZURV): to arrange for something to be kept for you to use later

shelter (SHEL-tur): something like a tent that protects you from the weather

strategic (struh-TEE-jik): carefully planned by thinking ahead

trace (trays): a sign that someone has been in a place; evidence

wilderness (WIL-dur-nis): wild land where no people live

wildlife (WILDE-life): wild animals living in their natural environment

Thinking Questions

1. What is backpacking?

2. What should you pack for backpacking?

3. Why is it important to take breaks while backpacking?

4. Where can you go backpacking?

5. What can you do to protect wildlife?

Index

About the Author

Madison Parker spent her childhood in the city of Chicago, Illinois. A farm girl at heart, today she lives in Wisconsin with her husband and four children on a small farm with cows, goats, chickens, and two miniature horses named Harley and David. Her favorite dessert is vanilla frozen custard with rainbow sprinkles, even in the winter.